DATE DUE

To librarians, because Jerome is their patron saint

*"For I bless God in the libraries of the learned and for all the booksellers
in the world."*

Jubilate Agno, Christopher Smart (1722–1771)

—M. H.

*And for Madeline, whom I love all the more
for her kindness to animals.*

—B. M.

ST.  EROME

AND THE LION

Retold by Margaret Hodges

Illustrated by Barry Moser

ORCHARD BOOKS · *New York*

Orchard Books
A division of Franklin Watts, Inc.
387 Park Avenue South
New York, NY 10016

Library of Congress Cataloging-in-Publication Data
Hodges, Margaret.
St. Jerome and the lion / retold by Margaret Hodges ;
illustrated by Barry Moser.   p.   cm.
Summary: An illustrated retelling of the legend of Saint Jerome
and the lion that he sheltered in his monastery.
ISBN 0-531-05938-3.
ISBN 0-531-08538-4 (lib.)
1. Jerome, Saint, d. 419 or 20—Legends—Juvenile literature.
[1. Jerome, Saint, d. 419 or 20.   2. Saints.]   I. Moser, Barry,
ill.   II. Title.
BR1720.J5H63   1991
270.2'092—dc20   90-22142
2   4   6   8   10   9   7   5   3   1

ST. JEROME AND THE LION

The legend of Saint Jerome and the lion was recorded in a Latin manuscript of the Middle Ages and is found in Jacques Paul Migne's *Patrologiae*, volume 22, column 209 ff. A translation is included in Helen Waddell's *Beasts and Saints*, published by Constable and Company, Ltd., London, 1934.

In one of Albrecht Dürer's engravings, *St. Jerome in His Cell*, the lion sleeps with the dog. A mural by Carpaccio in the church of San Giorgio di Schiavoni in Venice illustrates the arrival of the lion, with the monks in full flight. A second mural shows the death of Jerome, surrounded by the monks. He lies in the courtyard, while the dog on a leash barks at the grieving lion and the donkey grazes without a care in the world.

—M. H.

COULD never tell all that is remembered about Saint Jerome, that great man who lived long, long ago in the little town of Bethlehem. But I will tell you one story that has come down from those old days, never forgotten, because it seemed like a miracle, because of the lion.

Bethlehem was a holy place. King David had lived there, and there the infant Jesus had been born. Jerome built a monastery on the hill where the town stood, and monks gathered around him, living like brothers with Jerome as their father. Behind the white walls each had a narrow cell, and each had a task to do.

One cooked the soup; one baked the bread; one tended the grape vines and olive trees. Some plowed the monastery fields, sowed the wheat, and gathered in the harvest. Even the animals had work, suited to their natures. The dog was ready to bark and growl if strangers came to the gate. The hens laid eggs; the sheep gave wool for the monks' robes; and the donkey went with one of the brothers to bring back baskets of firewood.

As for Jerome, he governed the monastery by day and at night worked late at his desk. He was translating the Bible into Latin, the language understood by most people who could read. The work was long and hard.

Always at Jerome's side was the faithful dog, following him about or lying at his feet in the long hours of the night.

One evening, just as the brothers were about to sit down to their supper, they heard furious barking in the courtyard, and in rushed the dog, running to Jerome, pawing his knees, tugging at his robe. As Jerome followed the dog, the brothers left the table and peered fearfully out into the courtyard.

Through the open gateway came a great lion. He opened his mouth and roared. Away went the brothers, fleeing for their lives. Who could blame them? Some ran into their cells, some into the chapel. The dog trembled at the huge open mouth and sharp teeth of the lion. He hid himself behind Jerome's robes.

But Jerome did not run for safety. He saw that the lion was limping on three paws and

holding up the fourth paw as if in pain. The blessed Jerome went to meet him as one goes to greet a guest.

The lion could not speak, since it was not his nature, but he came forward and showed Jerome his wounded paw. It was full of thorns, and was swollen and feverish. Jerome called the brothers to come with warm water and clean cloths and healing herbs. Then he pulled out the thorns, while the lion looked gratefully into his face and tried not to howl.

When the paw healed, the lion became gentle as a lamb. The brothers gave him a cell, its floor covered with clean straw, and fed him their own food as if he were a brother, too. His coat grew thick and glossy. When the monks said their prayers, he listened for Jerome's voice, and he followed as Jerome went about his daily tasks. At night he lay by

Jerome's desk, his golden eyes watching the pen move across the paper, page after page. But the dog was suspicious. To him, the lion was an enemy, who had taken his place.

When at last the brothers turned the lion free to go back to his own wild world, he would not go.

"He cannot stay," said one brother. "The Bible says that the lion shall eat straw, but this one eats more meat than we do, and he does no work. What work can a lion do?"

But another said, "He could guard our donkey when she grazes in the forest pasture."

"Let him stay," said Jerome. "God could have healed the lion's paw without our help. He must have sent His creature to us for our good. In time, we shall know why."

So it was agreed. The lion learned to take

the donkey to pasture and to watch over her until evening, when he saw her safely home. Only the dog was discontented, and few visitors came to the gates since word had got about that the brothers kept a lion.

Then one hot day, while the donkey was at pasture, the lion fell asleep, tired out with too many late-night vigils in Jerome's study. And while he slept, the donkey wandered away down the monastery path to the main road where travelers passed by.

It happened that merchants, men from the East, were taking camels along the road, loaded with carpets and spices to trade in Egypt. The merchants wanted a donkey to lead their camels, as was the custom, but they had none. When they saw the monastery donkey, unguarded, they took her away with them. In a word, they stole her.

Too late the lion awoke. In vain he searched the forest pasture. The donkey was nowhere to be seen. Night fell, and still the lion stalked the fields and forests in deep distress, seeking the lost donkey. At last he gave up hope. He returned to the monastery and lay down at the gate, too sad and ashamed to go in for his supper.

The brothers found him there without the donkey, and thought the worst.

"Our food is not enough for you," said one young monk, who was always hungry himself. "You have killed our donkey. Go! Finish her off, but never come here again."

Jerome sent some of the brothers with lamps, to look for the donkey, alive or dead, but they found nothing.

When they brought home this news, Jerome spoke. "Brothers, we have lost our don-

key. But do not nag at the lion and make him miserable. He is sorry enough. Let him stay. Feed him as before. Only he must work. And since we have no donkey, the lion can take her place. Make a harness for him to wear and let him do the donkey's work. He will bring home our firewood."

The brothers agreed that this was only fair. So it was done. The king of beasts became a beast of burden. He bowed his head and let the brothers strap a harness on his back. Each day, he trotted obediently to the forest and dragged home loads of wood for the kitchen fires. But his heart was sore. His coat grew thin and dull.

He did not enter Jerome's study. The dog, seeing this, took his old place there, while the lion prowled about the forest pasture, hoping against hope to find the scent of the donkey. But it was long gone.

Summer passed, and winter came. Late one day, his work done, the lion returned to the pasture. Up and down, here and there, he ran, seeking some clue to the donkey's fate. Why he went at that time, I do not know. What inspired him can only be guessed.

At last, weary but too anxious to give up, the lion climbed a little hill from which he could see along the highway. Far in the distance, he saw merchants and a long line of camels loaded with goods. A donkey led this caravan by a halter tied to the first camel.

The lion leaped into the road. He ran to meet them. He had found his donkey. And never was there heard such a roar, as he raced toward her. The merchants left their camels and scrambled to hide in the hedges and hollows.

But the lion, dropping his roar to a growl,

did no harm. He herded the animals to the monastery gate, where the noise made the brothers look out. They were amazed to see their donkey leading the camels with the lion bringing up the rear, and they ran to tell Jerome.

"Open the gate," he said. "Relieve our guests of their burdens. Feed them, and wash their feet—our donkey and the camels too. Then let us prepare a meal for other guests who will soon arrive, hungry. We must be ready to welcome them."

The lion ran from one brother to another, lying flat at the feet of each one and trying to wag his tail like a dog, as if to say, "Forgive me for falling asleep on guard. I did not eat the donkey, but I forgive you for suspecting me."

"God has taught us a lesson," said Jerome.

"Here is our trusty friend, proved innocent by a miracle. We had judged him guilty without proof."

That night the lion and the dog lay down to rest, side by side, at Jerome's feet. Suddenly the dog barked, and a brother opened the gate. There were the merchants, travel-worn and fearful. When Jerome came forward, they threw themselves at his feet and begged forgiveness for stealing the donkey.

But Jerome raised them up gently and said, "Enjoy what is your own, my friends. Only do not take what belongs to others. God is always with us and sees what we do. Now, before you go on your way, rest and be welcome at our table."

The merchants answered, "Father, accept half the oil that our camels have brought from Egypt, for all these things must have hap-

pened so that we can fill the needs of your monastery."

"Not so," Jerome replied. "That would be a hardship for you. We are more blessed by giving than by taking."

"Do as we ask," the merchants begged. "We and our children's children will come to Bethlehem each year with a gift of oil to light your lamps so that all will remember this good day." They would not sit down to supper until Jerome had granted their wish. When they had eaten, he blessed them and their camels, and they went on their way, rejoicing, to their own country.

Almost two thousand years have passed since then. Jerome is Saint Jerome, famous for the Bible that he translated into Latin so long ago in Bethlehem. And wherever his story is told or his picture painted, the lion is with him, as he always wanted to be.

Manufactured in the United States of America
Printed by General Offset Company, Inc.
Bound by Horowitz/Rae
Book design by Barry Moser

The text of this book is set in 16 point Plantin.

The calligraphy is the work of Reassurance Wunder, based on an initial drawn
in 1491 by Guy Marchant.

The illustrations are transparent watercolors, painted on paper made at the
Barcham Green Mills, Hayle, G.B.